30·60

Life on a Civil War Battlefield

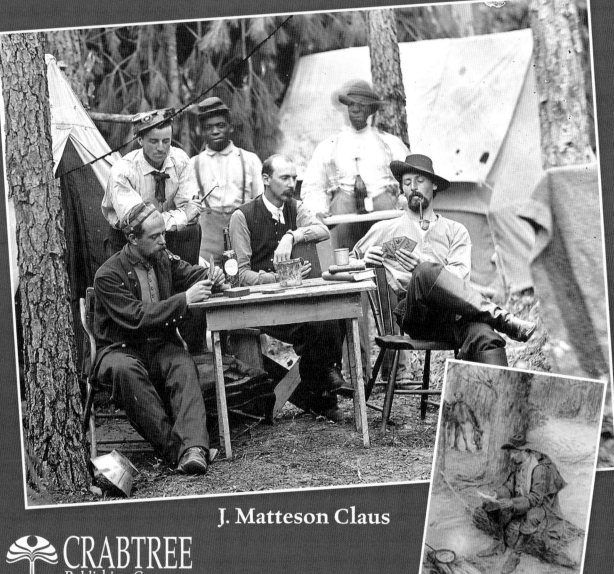

J. Matteson Claus

CRABTREE
Publishing Company
www.crabtreebooks.com

UNDERSTANDING THE CIVIL WAR

Author: J. Matteson Claus
Publishing plan research and development:
  Sean Charlebois, Reagan Miller
  Crabtree Publishing Company
Editors: Mark Cheatham, Kirsten Holm, Lynn Peppas
Proofreader: Wendy Scavuzzo
Editorial director: Kathy Middleton
Production coordinator: Shivi Sharma
Creative director: Arka Roy Chaudhary
Design: Sandy Kent
Cover design: Samara Parent
Photo research: Iti Shrotriya
Maps: Paul Brinkdopke
Production coordinator: Margaret Amy Salter
Prepress technician: Margaret Amy Salter
Print coordinator: Katherine Berti

Written, developed, and produced by Planman Technologies

Photographs and Reproductions
Front Cover: Photo © Christie's Images/Bridgeman Art Library; Title Page (p. 1): Library of Congress (top), The Granger Collection, New York. Table of Contents (p. 3): Chapter 1: Bettmann/CORBIS/Click Photos, Chapter 2: North Wind / North Wind Picture Archives, Chapter 3: CORBIS/Click Photos, Chapter 4: Library of Congress, Chapter 5: North Wind / North Wind Picture Archives. Chapter Opener image (pp. 5, 13, 21, 32, 39): North Wind / North Wind Picture Archives

Bettmann/CORBIS/Click Photos, p. 9, The Mariners' Museum/CORBIS/Click Photos, p. 26, CORBIS/Click Photos, p. 28 (top), Bettmann/CORBIS/Click Photos, p. 28 (center); The Granger Collection, New York: pp. 10, 42; Library of Congress: pp. 4, 7 (bottom), 11, 13, 16, 17, 22, 29, 30, 33, 34, 36 (top and bottom), 37 (top, center, bottom), 38 (left and right); Mary Evans Picture Library / Alamy, 28 (bottom left); North Wind / North Wind Picture Archives, pp. 8, 19, 28 (bottom right), 41; Peter Newark Military Pictures/Photolibrary, p. 7 (top); The Print Collector/Photolibrary, p. 12; Thinkstock, p. 43 (top), Photodisc/Thinkstock, p. 43 (bottom); Idanbury/BigStock, p. 44.
Page 25 (top to bottom): Springfield musket rifle, model 1861 (wood & metal) by American School, (19th century) Private Collection/ Photo © Civil War Archive/ The Bridgeman Art Library; Springfield rifle, 1826 (wood & metal) by American School, (19th century) Gettysburg National Military Park Museum, Pennsylvania, USA/ Photo © Civil War Archive/ The Bridgeman Art Library; 1853 Pattern Rifled Musket (Enfield rifle), 1855 (wood & metal) by English School, (19th century) Royal Armouries, Leeds, UK/ The Bridgeman Art Library; INTERFOTO / Alamy; Colt Navy revolver from the N.C. Infantry, 1851 (wood & metal) by American School, (19th century) Private Collection/ Photo © Civil War Archive/ The Bridgeman Art Library

Front cover: Two Union soldiers rest at their camp during a break in battle.
Back cover (background): A military map of the United States from 1862 shows forts and military posts.
Back cover (logo): A civil war era cannon stands in front of the flag from Fort Sumter.
Title page (top): Union soldiers playing cards in camp at Petersburg, Virginia
Title page (bottom): A Confederate cavalryman reads a letter from home.

Library and Archives Canada Cataloguing in Publication

Claus, J. Matteson, 1969-
  Life on a Civil War battlefield / J. Matteson Claus.

(Understanding the Civil War)
Includes index.
Issued also in electronic formats.
ISBN 978-0-7787-5340-7 (bound).--ISBN 978-0-7787-5357-5 (pbk.)

  1. United States--History--Civil War, 1861-1865--Social aspects--Juvenile literature. 2. United States. Army--History--Civil War, 1861-1865--Juvenile literature. 3. United States. Army--Military life--History--19th century-- Juvenile literature. 4. Confederate States of America. Army--History--Juvenile literature. 5. Confederate States of America. Army--Military life--Juvenile literature. 6. Soldiers--United States--History--19th century--Juvenile literature. 7. Soldiers--Confederate States of America--History--Juvenile literature. I. Title. II. Series: Understanding the Civil War

E607.C53 2011   j973.7'83   C2011-907475-3

Library of Congress Cataloging-in-Publication Data

Claus, J. Matteson, 1969-
  Life on a Civil War battlefield / J. Matteson Claus.
    p. cm. -- (Understanding the Civil War)
  Includes index.
  ISBN 978-0-7787-5340-7 (reinforced library binding : alk. paper) --
  ISBN 978-0-7787-5357-5 (pbk. : alk. paper) -- ISBN 978-1-4271-9939-3 (electronic pdf) -- ISBN 978-1-4271-9948-5 (electronic html)
  1. United States. Army--History--Civil War, 1861-1865--Juvenile literature. 2. Confederate States of America. Army--History--Juvenile literature. 3. United States. Army--Military life--History--19th century--Juvenile literature. 4. Confederate States of America. Army--Military life--Juvenile literature. 5. Soldiers--United States--History--19th century--Juvenile literature. 6. Soldiers-- Confederate States of America--Juvenile literature. I. Title.
  E607.C59 2011
  973.7--dc23

2011045079

Crabtree Publishing Company

www.crabtreebooks.com   1-800-387-7650

Printed in the U.S.A./112011/JA20111018

Published in Canada
Crabtree Publishing
616 Welland Ave.
St. Catharines, Ontario
L2M 5V6

Published in the United States
Crabtree Publishing
PMB 59051
350 Fifth Avenue, 59th Floor
New York, New York 10118

Published in the United Kingdom
Crabtree Publishing
Maritime House
Basin Road North, Hove
BN41 1WR

Published in Australia
Crabtree Publishing
3 Charles Street
Coburg North
VIC 3058

TABLE *of* CONTENTS

> *War loses a great deal of romance after a soldier has seen his first battle. . . It is a classical maxim that it is sweet and becoming to die for one's country; but whoever has seen the horrors of a battle-field feels that it is far sweeter to live for it.*
>
> —from *Mosby's War Reminiscences* by John S. Mosby

This romantic vision of battle is from a music cover entitled "The Two Standard Bearers: The Day After the Battle." It shows a wounded Union soldier and a fallen Confederate soldier, each grasping their flag.

Who Fought in the Civil War?

The American Civil War was fought from April 12, 1861 to May 13, 1865. During those four years, almost every American family had relatives and friends fighting in the war.

The Military at the Beginning of the War

More than three million soldiers fought during the war. The Union army employed about 2.2 million soldiers. About 900,000 soldiers fought for the Confederacy.

The Army

Neither the Union nor the Confederacy were ready for a war. When the war began in 1861, the United States military belonged to the Union. The army had only 16,000 men. Most of these troops were stationed west of the Mississippi. They were not located in the East where war was breaking out. When states began to **secede**, about a third of these troops left the Union to join the Confederacy.

> *The North cannot subdue us. We are too determined to be free. . .If by power of overwhelming numbers they conquer us, it will be a barren victory over a desolate land.*
>
> —Sarah Morgan Dawson, *Confederate Girl's Diary*

Major Events

1861

March
Confederate Congress authorizes 100,000 volunteer army

April
Civil War begins
Lincoln authorizes 75,000 volunteer army

1862

April
Confederate Conscription Act

1863

March
Union Conscription Act

July
New York City Draft Riots

December
Confederate Congress abolishes substitutes

1864

July
Union Congress repeals commutation

1865

May 13
Civil War ends

The Confederacy began to call for volunteers earlier than the Union. At the beginning of the war, the number of troops fighting for the Confederacy and the Union were almost evenly matched. However, that quickly changed. By 1862, the Union army had an average of 2.5 soldiers for every Confederate soldier.

Navy

The U.S. Navy was also unprepared for war. The navy had about 90 ships, but only 14 were ready to put to sea in early 1861. Within a year, though, the navy boasted of 300 new warships. In addition, the Navy did not lose as many sailors to the Confederacy. Only a small percentage of the seamen left to join the South.

The Confederate military began the war with no navy. The warships and most of the shipyards were located in the North. The South quickly set about creating a navy. Most Confederate shipyards were captured from the Union.

Building an Army

In 1861, both the Union and the Confederacy built up their armies with volunteers. The majority of these men had no military training. Even the officers were often inexperienced.

Southern Volunteers

The Confederate Congress called for 100,000 volunteers on March 6, 1861. Many of these volunteers came from local **militia** units. These first Confederate volunteers were expected to **enlist** for one year. In 1862, however, many of these men had their enlistments extended for another two years.

Northern Volunteers

In April 1861, President Lincoln called for 75,000 volunteers. By this time, the Confederacy already had about 60,000 volunteers. The first Union volunteers enlisted for 90 days. When it became clear that the war would not be won in three months, the enlistment period was changed. On May 3, Lincoln called for more troops. These troops enlisted for 3 years. Some of the 90-day troops enlisted for another 3 years when their 90 days were up.

🌠 What Do You Know!

A SOLDIER BY ANY OTHER NAME
Both Union and Confederate soldiers had many names for each other.

CONFEDERATE
Reb, Rebel, or Johnny Reb; Southern soldier; Grey Backs; Secesh.

UNION
Yank, Yankee, or Billy Yank; Federal, Union, or Northern soldier; Bluebellies; Little Coot.

Then, in July, Congress authorized another one million troops. Again, the term was for three years. Some states, however, only required their volunteers to enlist for two years.

The Confederate States of America issued its own currency.

Pay

Both the North and South were supposed to pay their volunteers every two months. This did not usually happen. Troops moved around a lot so it was difficult for the paymaster to catch up with them. Many soldiers kept some of their pay and sent the rest home to help their families.

Monthly Army Pay		
	Confederate	*Union*
Private	$11.00	$13.00
Corporal	$13.00	$13.00
Sergeant	$17.00	$17.00
Captain	$130.00	$115.00
Major	$150.00	$169.00
Colonel	$195.00	$212.00

Source: CivilWar.org

What the Army Looked Like

Since the armies consisted of volunteers at the start of the war, both Union and Confederate army units were often made up of men from the same areas. Men who lived in towns near each other would join together to form **companies** (100 men) and **regiments** (10 companies). Often, members of the same family would serve together in the same unit.

As a result, many companies had strong community ties. While this was good for **morale**, it also had a major drawback. If a unit suffered a lot of **casualties**, many men from the same town or same family could be injured, captured, or killed at the same time.

Age

At the beginning of the war, the enlistment age was usually 18–45. Most soldiers were aged between 18 and 30 years of age. Later in the war, older and younger men also joined. The average age of the Union soldiers was 25 years, but about 40 percent were 21 or younger. The average soldier was a young, white, single, Protestant, and had been born in the United States.

In both armies, the minimum fighting age of a soldier was 18. Yet, younger boys found ways to join both sides. Sometimes boys would join as musicians, such as buglers or drummer boys.

Drummer boy in Union uniform

Immigrants

Immigrants played an important part in the war. Twenty-five percent of the Union soldiers were immigrants. In the South, almost ten percent of the soldiers were immigrants. At first, immigrant soldiers were the cause of some conflict. There was some prejudice against the different immigrant groups. Language differences also made communication difficult, but immigrants were eventually accepted.

In some cases, immigrants blended in with other troops. Sometimes they had their own groups. There were whole companies made up of one ethnic group such as German, Irish, or Hispanic soldiers.

African Americans

At the beginning of the war, African Americans were not allowed to fight for either the North or the South. This was illegal until 1862 when the North began to allow African Americans to enlist. By the end of the war, more than 180,000 African-American soldiers had served in the army. This was about 10 percent of Union soldiers.

In contrast, the South did not allow African Americans to enlist until 1865. The war was over before this new law went into effect. Some Confederate soldiers brought slaves along with them to work as cooks or laborers. Most enslaved people, however, were left at home to continue working.

Native Americans

Native Americans fought for both the Union and the Confederate armies. The Union had three Native American regiments called the Indian Home Guard. The Confederates had three **brigades** of Native Americans.

Why Fight?

As soon as the war began, thousands of men volunteered to fight. What motivated them? For one thing, both sides thought that they would win quickly. Some soldiers even worried that the war would be over before they got a chance to fight. Many soldiers looked at fighting in the war as an adventure and a chance to join in some fun.

Each side thought it was superior to the other. Though outnumbered, the Confederates thought they would easily beat the Union. At the same

People in the War

Stand Watie

A leader of the Cherokee, Stand Watie lived in what is now Oklahoma. Watie organized a regiment of Native Americans to fight for the South. His troops fought in many battles, including Wilson's Creek and Pea Ridge. In 1864, Watie was promoted to brigadier general. He commanded the First Indian Brigade. On June 23, 1865, he surrendered to the North, the last Confederate general to admit defeat.

> *Lincoln may bring his 75,000 troops against us. We fight for our homes, our fathers and mothers, our wives, brothers, sisters, sons, and daughters!*
>
> —Confederate Vice President Alexander H. Stephens, April 22, 1861

time, the Union soldiers thought they could beat the Confederates just as easily.

Men from the South fought for states' rights and the right to secede. They did not want to be part of a country that might outlaw slavery, which would threaten them economically. They also fought to defend their homes and families.

Men from the North fought to preserve the Union of the United States. They did not think that certain states should tear apart the Union. Men on both sides fought out of a sense of patriotism. They believed in their cause.

Slavery

At the beginning of the war, ending slavery was not the main goal of the Union. Slavery was still legal in several Union states. The North went to war to keep the Southern states from seceding from the Union. Only later did Lincoln abolish slavery and bring the issue to the forefront.

TO ARMS!
RALLY FOR THE RIGHT!
Recruits Wanted
FOR THREE MONTHS SERVICE, IN
COMPANY A
GRAY RESERVES
CAPT. CHARLES S. SMITH.
ARMORY,
810 MARKET STREET,
UP STAIRS.

Union army draft poster, Philadelphia, 1862

Brother Against Brother

Differing views about the war divided some families. The war literally pitted brother against brother. For example, James and Alexander Campbell were brothers. But they fought on opposite sides of the war. One day, they found themselves on opposite sides during the same battle.

> *I have served my country under the flag of the Union for more than fifty years, and as long as God permits me to live, I will defend that flag with my sword; even if my own native State assails [attacks] it.*
>
> —Union General and Virginian Winfield Scott, April 21, 1861

A Confederate cavalryman reads a letter from home

James wrote about the battle,

"I was astonished to hear… that you was color Bearer of the Regmt that assaulted the Battery… I was in the Brest work during the whole engagement doing my Best to Beat you. but I hope you and I will never again meet face to face bitter enemies on the Battlefield. but if such should be the case You've but to discharge your duty for your cause for I can assure you I will strive to discharge my duty to my country and my cause."

Alexander wrote to his wife,

"It is rather bad to think that we should be fighting him on the one side and me on the other for he says he was in the fort during the whole engagement. I hope to god that he and I will get safe through it all and he will have his story to tell about his side and I will have my story to tell about my side."

The Campbells are just one example of what many families faced. Even the first family was affected. Mary Todd Lincoln, the President's wife, had relatives who fought for the Confederate army.

Conscription

At first, volunteers were enough to fill both armies. At the start of the war, both armies had more soldiers than they could provide for. Some were turned away because there were not enough supplies to outfit all who volunteered. As the war dragged on, the armies needed more troops. Both sides passed **conscription** laws. These laws were very unpopular.

Confederate Conscription

By 1862, the Confederate army did not have enough soldiers. As a result, it passed the Confederate Conscription Act on April 16, 1862. This was the first conscription law in U.S. history. The law said that all able-bodied white men aged 18–35 were eligible for the **draft**. If drafted, these men were required to serve for three years. The law also affected volunteers

🌠 What Do You Know!

LETTERS AND DIARIES
Much of what we know about the Civil War comes from letters and diaries. As with the Campbells' letters, these first-person accounts give detailed information about what life was like. Letters were the main way for soldiers to communicate. For example, in the Union army, about 45,000 letters were sent each day in the East. About 90,000 were sent daily in the West.

who had already enlisted. They had agreed to serve for one year. Now, they were required to serve for two more years.

There were ways around the draft. Men who worked at certain jobs, or occupations, were **exempted**. Also, a man who was drafted could pay a **substitute** to go to war in his place. Substitutes were usually immigrants or men who were older or younger than the enlistment age. This allowed the rich to buy their way out of the war. It also allowed the poor to make money working as a substitute. By 1863, some substitutes earned as much as $6,000. That was equal to three years wages. In 1863, the Confederate Congress stopped allowing substitutes.

Southerners didn't like the draft. They avoided the draft officers. Some who were too poor to buy their way out would run away and hide. Others would take up arms against the draft officers.

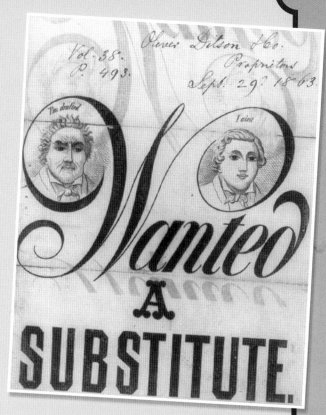

This sheet music cover protests the unfairness of the Southern draft. A drafted man could supply a substitute instead of reporting for service. The captions above the two faces read "I'm drafted" and "I ain't."

Union Conscription

By 1863, the Union was also facing a lack of soldiers. About 130 regiments had served their time and were due to go home. In March 1863, Congress passed a Conscription Act. Able-bodied men between the ages of 20–45 were eligible for the draft. In July 1863, the first draft was held. Three more drafts occurred in 1864. Draftees had many ways to avoid the draft. In fact, only about seven percent of the men who were drafted actually served.

Unlike the South, there were no exemptions for occupation. As in the South, men in the North could hire a substitute. The Union army also allowed men to pay a fee instead of serving. This was called **commutation**. The fee was $300, equal to about a year's wages for the average person. Commutation favored the rich, which made it very unpopular. Congress finally did away with commutation in 1864.

Bounties were payments made by cities, states, and eventually the federal government to get men to join. The Union only drafted men from an area if it hadn't filled its quota of volunteers. So, areas used

After the Conscription Act was passed, riots broke out in many Northern cities. This picture shows police trying to control rioters in New York City.

bounties to get men to volunteer and avoid the need for the draft. This helped persuade the Union to allow African Americans to fight, since they would help fill a quota.

The draft was hugely unpopular in the North, as it was in the South. Many avoided it. Some men fled, bribed doctors to say they were unable to fight, pretended to be sick or insane, or even hurt themselves so they wouldn't be able to fight. The draft was particularly unpopular with immigrants and poorer people, who could not afford to pay the $300 commutation fee. In addition, white draftees feared that free African Americans would take their jobs while they were away fighting. Economic fears and racism combined to cause the worst riots in American history.

Riots broke out across the country, in Illinois, Wisconsin, Connecticut, New Hampshire, and New Jersey. The worst riots occurred in New York City. From July 13–17, a mob of largely Irish Catholic immigrants **rampaged** through the streets. They burned down the Colored Orphan Asylum and attacked and murdered African Americans. Several police stations and the property of **abolitionists** and Republicans were destroyed. More than 100 people were killed. Union troops were called in and fought the rioters to restore order. Despite the unrest and resentment, the draft remained in effect.

2 Everyday Life

Thousands of battles were fought during the Civil War, but most of a soldier's time was not spent on the battlefield. Soldiers might march for days or even weeks. They would make camp and wait until they received the order to fight. A battle might last a few hours or a few days. Then the process would start all over again.

Camp Life

In the Civil War, soldiers were constantly on the move. They spent a lot of time marching to battle sites. Soldiers marched great distances, through all kinds of **terrain** and in all kinds of weather. When they were not fighting or marching, soldiers stayed in **camps**.

Camp housing was **crude**. It was designed to be temporary and easily moved. This was practical since the troops moved around so much. Most of the year, soldiers slept outside on the ground or in tents.

> *The hardships of forced marches are often more painful than the dangers of battle.*
>
> —Confederate General Stonewall Jackson

Sketch of a Union camp near Upperville, Virginia, 1862

Union soldiers often slept in canvas **dog tents**. Confederate soldiers slept in canvas tents when they were available. When soldiers did not have tents, they invented their own shelters. They hung bushes, oilcloths, and overcoats over four posts to create cover. These shelters were called **shebangs**.

During the winter, there was little fighting so soldiers stayed in one place for longer periods. As a result, winter camps sometimes had more permanent shelters such as wooden cabins and huts. These were warmer than sleeping in tents. Sometimes soldiers dug a hole in the ground and added a roof. These were called **bombproofs**. In the spring, the wood from these buildings could be used for firewood.

Clothing

At first, both armies wore a mix of clothing, in a variety of colors and styles. This caused problems on the battlefield. Soldiers could not tell friend from foe. They accidentally shot the wrong people or let enemies go.

Uniforms became standardized by the end of 1861. The Union uniforms were blue. The Confederates wore gray uniforms. Later, they also wore brown.

Still, some officers were known for their highly personal style of clothing. Union Major General George Custer was a snappy dresser, favoring a black vest and red neckerchief. Confederate Brigadier General John Hunt Morgan adopted the clothing style of early Virginia cavaliers from the late 1600s. He wore a black cape with red lining, knee-high boots, large gloves, and an ostrich-plumed hat.

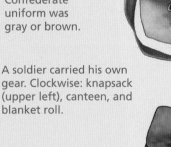

Confederate soldier
At the beginning of the war, volunteers wore many different colors and styles of uniforms. Eventually the Union uniform was blue. The Confederate uniform was gray or brown.

A soldier carried his own gear. Clockwise: knapsack (upper left), canteen, and blanket roll.

Typical personal grooming items included a comb, soap, razor, and toothbrush.

Necessary Items

Since soldiers moved a lot and marched great distances, they carried as little as possible. Soldiers, however, did carry a few essentials with them in a **knapsack**. Extra food was carried in a canvas bag called a **haversack**.

Shortages

As the war progressed, both armies faced some shortages, but the Confederacy faced more shortages than the Union. Gray cloth became scarce in the South so soldiers wore uniforms made of a homespun cloth dyed a brownish color. These were called "**butternuts**" because butternut shells were used in the dye. Uniforms were scarce, but shoes were even harder to find. Sometimes soldiers went barefoot. In fact, it is estimated that one-third of the Confederate army went barefoot during the war.

Union soldier
Soldiers carried muskets or rifles and ammunition. Cartridges were carried in a special case.

A soldier might carry family photographs, stamps, paper, a pen, and envelopes for writing letters, and money he did not send home.

Soldiers often cooked their own food on small campfires. Coffee was made in a pot to share and drunk from tin mugs.

> *…after each fight I would search the field for anyone near my size who did not require use of his equipment. I must confess to feeling very bad doing this, believing the dead should not be disturbed… but I had no other course.*
>
> —Alabama soldier, Abel Sheeks

People in the War

**John Clem,
The Drummer Boy
of Chickamauga**

John Clem was the youngest soldier to become a noncommissioned officer in the U.S. Army. He was almost ten years old when he tried to join the Union army in 1861. At first, he had no luck. He eventually convinced the 22nd Michigan to bring him along. He became their mascot and unofficial drummer boy. In 1863, he was allowed to enlist. Clem fought at Horseshoe Ridge, where he fought bravely and refused to surrender. As a result, he was promoted to sergeant.

Soldiers made up for shortages in supplies however they could. After battles, the survivors would sometimes loot the dead bodies for shoes, uniforms, and other supplies.

Camp Activities

A soldier's day generally ran from 5:00 A.M. to 9:00 P.M. While in camp, the majority of the day was spent **drilling**. Drills helped to train the soldiers. Drilling taught them how to use their weapons, march, and follow orders. It also helped to build team spirit.

With only drilling to keep them occupied, soldiers became bored. This lowered their morale. Homesickness was also a problem. Once the grim realities of war set in, soldiers often found themselves longing for home.

To keep the soldiers' spirits up, entertainment was very important in the camps. Group singing was a common activity in Civil War times. Soldiers would get together and sing everything from hymns to popular songs. Some units had musicians such as drummers and buglers. Also, some regular soldiers brought musical instruments with them. Portable instruments such as banjos and harmonicas were popular because they were easy to carry.

Soldiers amused themselves by playing games. The most popular game was playing cards. If soldiers did not have cards, they would make their own decks. They also played board games, such as checkers and chess.

Soldiers played more physical games, too. These included boxing, wrestling, playing baseball, and footraces. In the winter, soldiers went sledding and ice-skating. They also built snowmen and had snowball fights.

> *The first thing in the morning is drill, then drill, then drill again. Then drill, drill, a little more drill. Then drill and lastly drill. Between drills we drill and sometimes stop to eat a little and have role-call.*
>
> —Private Oliver Norton

With so much time on their hands, letter writing became hugely important to the soldiers. It was their only communication with home. They looked forward to getting mail and would reread their letters over and over.

In addition to letters, soldiers read books and newspapers. If they did not have anything to read, sometimes they would create their own newspapers and pass them around the camps.

Religion was very important to soldiers in the Civil War. Soldiers read a lot of religious materials, particularly Bibles and religious pamphlets. Some soldiers carried their own Bibles. Free copies were also available.

Soldiers also found other ways to amuse themselves. The military did not always approve of these pastimes. Gambling was extremely popular. Men gambled on just about everything. They gambled on games such as cards and dice, board games, and different kinds of races. Smoking was also popular. Both the Confederacy and Union gave out tobacco as part of the soldiers' **rations**. Sometimes the soldiers were also issued alcohol. Until September 1862, Navy enlisted men were given a specific amount of wine or grog (beer and water) each day. The military tried to restrict alcohol, but soldiers bought it anyway or made it themselves.

> *I found one crying this morning. I tried to comfort him but had hard work to keep from joining him.*
>
> —Captain Harley Wayne

 What Do You Know!

LICE

Lice were unwelcome members of the camps and soldiers were plagued by them. As a result, the soldiers developed all sorts of lice-related slang.

Lice were called "Bragg's bodyguard," after General Bragg, and sometimes "Gray Backs," which was also a cruel term for Rebel soldiers.

"Fighting under the black flag" meant killing lice while "giving the vermin a parole" meant throwing away clothing that was overrun by lice.

Sometimes men were so bored that even the lice became a source of entertainment. Men in both armies held louse races!

Union soldiers playing cards in camp at Petersburg, Virginia

Food

Union soldiers ate **hardtack**. This was a square cracker made out of flour, water, and salt. The salt helped keep some bugs out of the hardtack. The soldiers called hardtack "worm castles" because it was often filled with weevil larvae. The cracker was very hard and did not taste very good. To make it edible, soldiers got creative. Recipes included dunking or crumbling it into coffee or soaking it in water and then frying it in fat.

Confederate soldiers did not usually eat hardtack unless they had taken it from Union soldiers. The main grain for Southern soldiers was cornmeal. This also attracted all kinds of vermin. The cornmeal was often made into a dry cornbread that was not very tasty. Soldiers also made cornmeal mush by mixing it with water. Hoecakes or ashcakes were made by mixing cornmeal with water and baking it. Like hardtack, these cakes traveled well.

Both sides also ate salt pork and bacon. Their other rations included dried peas, dried beans, soft bread, rice, sugar, salt, and vinegar. There were also some canned goods. These were more common among the officers and in the hospitals.

Soldiers had to have rations that would not spoil and would travel well. That meant that fresh meat, fruit, and vegetables were rare. Both sides would **forage** for food. Soldiers would also hunt to get fresh meat.

Coffee was an important part of the soldiers' diet. Union soldiers were given coffee as part of their rations, but Confederate soldiers did not have enough coffee. When they had to, they used things such as chicory and acorns to make a coffee substitute. Confederate soldiers would go to great lengths to get coffee, though. They would even cross enemy lines to trade for it.

HOPPIN' JOHN

1 lb dried black-eyed peas
3 pints cold water
½ lb sliced salt pork or bacon
1 tsp Tabasco sauce
½ tsp salt
2 tbsp bacon fat or lard
2 medium onions, chopped
1 c uncooked long-grain rice
1 ½ c boiling water

Cover peas with water. Soak overnight. Add salt pork, Tabasco, and salt. Cover and cook on low heat for 30 minutes. Meanwhile, cook onions in bacon fat till yellow. Then add peas, rice, and boiling water. Cook until tender and water is absorbed, about 20–25 minutes. Stir occasionally. Yield: about eight servings.

Hungry Soldiers

Soldiers on both sides of the war had trouble getting enough to eat. Their diets were not varied enough to provide good nutrition.

This was harmful to the soldiers. Malnutrition contributed to sickness and death. During the summer and fall, soldiers often had plenty to eat. In the winter and spring, however, food became scarce.

Union troops were usually well-supplied by federal quartermasters whose job it was to give out supplies and provisions. The food troops received was not always edible, though. When supply lines were broken, soldiers were ordered to "live off the land."

Confederate soldiers did not fare so well. Union blockades caused food shortages. Southern farms became scarred battlefields where no crops could be grown. By the end of the war, food was so scarce that some Confederate soldiers starved to death. In desperation, they sometimes ate anything they could find, including dogs, cats, and rats.

Soldiers frequently cooked their own food. As a result, they often carried cooking equipment with them. Otherwise, they used their bayonets to roast meat. They might also attach wire handles to tin cans and use them as pots.

Union soldiers cooking over a campfire

Killer Camps

The main cause of soldiers' deaths during the Civil War was from disease, not wounds from fighting. Over 620,000 soldiers died in the Civil War. It is estimated that about two-thirds of these deaths were caused from disease. Camp conditions were partly responsible.

Cleanliness

Hygiene was an issue in the camps. People did not realize the importance of cleanliness. Soldiers were not able to wash every day. They were infested with lice and they used the same pots for cooking food that they used to boil the lice out of their clothing.

What Do You Know!

SCURVY

Scurvy is a disease caused by a lack of vitamin C. Symptoms of scurvy include soft gums, loose teeth, bleeding sores, and wounds that do not heal. If untreated, it leads to death from heart damage and internal bleeding.

Scurvy is often associated with sailors, but it was also a real problem for the army during the Civil War. The lack of fresh fruits and vegetables meant soldiers contracted scurvy. Soldiers did the best they could to combat the disease. They foraged for unusual sources of vitamin C, such as wild onions and sassafras buds. In the winter, when fresh produce was not available, they sometimes had dried fruits and vegetables to eat.

Not only were people dirty, but the camps themselves were filthy. Garbage piled up. **Latrines** built too close to water supplies could **contaminate** drinking water. Bugs were everywhere. Many bugs, such as lice and mosquitoes, carried diseases.

Diseases

With so many people in close contact, camps were a breeding ground for disease. Soldiers, particularly those from **rural** areas, came into contact with diseases they had never been exposed to before. Constant exposure to weather also lowered the soldiers' **immune systems**. In addition, poor diet weakened them.

A swarm of diseases resulted from these conditions. Some, such as measles and mumps, were not always fatal but could make an entire unit so sick that they were unable to fight for weeks. Other diseases, such as smallpox, were deadly. The most deadly killer in the war was **dysentery** or **diarrhea**. The second biggest killer was **typhoid fever**, which was spread by lice. Pneumonia was the third most common cause of death.

Civil War Deaths			
Union Enlistment	2,893,304	Confederate Enlistment	1,317,035
Battle Deaths	110,070	Battle Deaths	94,000
Disease Deaths	224,586	Disease Deaths	164,000
Other Causes	24,872	Other Causes	No record given
Total Deaths	359,528	Total Deaths	258,000
Percentage Deaths	12.4%	Percentage Deaths	19.8%

Source: *CivilWar.org. Statistics courtesy of the Museum of the Confederacy*

Combat

Civil War soldiers fought battles on land and sea. They fought in the South, North, East, and West. How and when the soldiers fought was determined by **military strategy**. Trial and error, politics, and public opinion greatly influenced military strategy in the North and South. Each side had its own governing ideas.

Union Strategy

The main political goal of the Union was to bring the Southern states back into the Union. Ending slavery was not part of the plan at first. Later on, it became an important goal.

The Union had three main military strategies to achieve its goals. A **blockade** of Southern ports would cut the South off from supplies. In the West, Union control of the Mississippi River would divide the Confederacy and cut off communications and supplies. The Union would defeat Confederate armies in Virginia and capture Richmond, the Confederate capital.

Confederate Strategy

The main political goal of the Confederacy was to become a separate nation. Southerners wanted to keep their way of life and **preserve** their cotton economy which was based on slavery. The North needed to conquer the South to achieve its goal. The South needed only to defend its territory until the North got tired of war and gave up. At that point, the South believed the North would agree to a peace treaty.

The South looked to European countries for assistance. Foreign recognition of the Confederacy as a separate country would help the South. In May 1861, Great Britain declared itself neutral—it would not take sides. France and Spain soon followed. The South continued its efforts to win recognition until the end of the war.

The Mississippi River was an essential transportation route for the South. This picture shows cotton and sugar being loaded onto ships in Memphis, Tennessee.

The South believed that it could use cotton to get what it wanted from Great Britain. Southern cotton provided more than 75 percent of the raw materials used by British textile mills. With the Union blockade, the supply of cotton dried up. The South hoped that Great Britain would pierce the Union blockade and bring supplies and arms to Confederate ports.

The South's efforts, however, were not successful. British mills turned to Egypt, India, and other sources for cotton. The Emancipation Proclamation in January 1863 dashed the South's hopes for good. The goal of freeing slaves in Confederate states made the war about ending slavery as well as saving the Union. Britain had outlawed slavery in 1833. The South would need to fight on alone.

Strengths and Weaknesses

The Union had many advantages over the Confederacy. It had more of almost everything, including food, factories, and railroads. It also had more men available to fight, more ships, and more arms. One of the North's greatest advantages was President Lincoln. He was smart, patient, and skillful.

The Union had disadvantages, too. The Union army had to invade the South, which was unfamiliar territory. The Union faced a very determined South. State militias and small bands of raiders attacked Union soldiers. Uncooperative civilians sympathized with Confederate soldiers. Early in the war, the Union army had tried to treat Southern civilians with respect. As the war continued, Union commanders were given permission to seize any property or supplies, and they took action against civilians giving aid to Confederate raiders.

The Confederacy had its own advantages. People in the South strongly supported the war. Since the war was fought mostly in the South, soldiers were on familiar ground. The soldiers were strongly motivated to defend their homes and lifestyle. The South also had a strong military tradition and was home to many military schools. Few enlisted men resigned from the U.S. Army to serve with the Confederate army. About one-third of U.S. Army officers resigned and became Confederate officers, however. Confederate generals such as Robert E. Lee, P.G.T. Beauregard, and Stonewall Jackson were graduates of West Point. They fought against many of their fellow graduates.

The South also had several disadvantages. It had fewer factories, weapons, ships, and railroads than the North. It also had fewer men to fight. Since it was a **confederation**, and not a union, state governors did not always send as many troops to fight in the army, keeping some men at home to keep their state safe. The South grew fewer food crops, since much of the land there was devoted to money-making crops such as cotton and rice. Throughout the war, the South was plagued by shortages of food and supplies.

What Do You Know!

DESERTERS

The North and South shared one disadvantage: they both had deserters. These were soldiers who left the war without permission.

Sometimes men went home to help their families or to visit and then return. But, most often, they did not return. Both armies tried to stop desertions through penalties that included fines, imprisonment, and even execution, but many men still deserted.

It is estimated that in both armies combined, up to 12,000 men deserted each month. Over the course of the war, it is estimated that about 300,000 men deserted.

The Army

The armies had various **ranks**. Most soldiers were privates, the lowest rank. The highest rank, the generals, made up the smallest portion of the army. Each branch of the army had its own **insignia** that corresponded to rank. The colors of the insignia showed what branch of the military the wearer belonged to: yellow for cavalry, sky blue for infantry, and red for **artillery**.

The Union had 16 armies, each named after a river, such as the Army of the Potomac. The Confederacy had 23 armies, each named after a state or region, such as the Army of Northern Virginia.

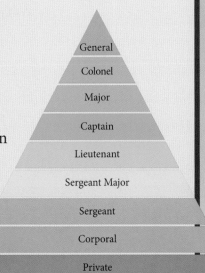

General
Colonel
Major
Captain
Lieutenant
Sergeant Major
Sergeant
Corporal
Private

Source: *Civilwar.org, Life at War*

Each army was split into groups:
- a company had 50–100 men
- a regiment had 10 companies
- a brigade had about 4 regiments
- a division had 2–5 brigades
- a corps had 2 or more divisions
- an army had 1 or more corps

While these were supposed to be the numbers of men in battle, disease often cut regiments in size by half. Most states did not send replacements to existing companies, preferring to form new companies instead.

Infantry and Cavalry

The **infantry** were the foot soldiers. They fought and traveled on foot. Their weapons and ammunition needed to be light enough for them to carry.

The **cavalry** were the soldiers on horseback. In the Civil War, the cavalry was mostly used for gathering information. Their advantage was that they could move quickly from one to place to another. If they fought, they would usually dismount and fight on foot. In that case, every fourth man became a "horse holder" and took the horses behind the battle lines.

ARMING THE CAVALRY

Cavalry weapons included Spencer carbines, six-shooter revolvers, and sabers. But the most important equipment for a cavalryman was his horse. Union soldiers were issued horses by the government. In contrast, Confederate soldiers usually owned their horses. If their horse was wounded or killed, it was their responsibility to replace it or they would be transferred to an infantry regiment. Soldiers were sometimes given 60 days leave to return home to get a new horse.

Weapons

Most arms manufacturing was done in the North, particularly in Springfield, Massachusetts. Other factories turned to making weapons according to government plans. Many weapons were purchased from England. The South had fewer factories and held fewer weapons at the start of the war. The Confederacy also got weapons by seizing federal weapons storehouses in seceding states. New factories in the South began making weapons, although they could not produce them as quickly or as well.

Civil War Insignia

Union Officers	Confederate Officers
General	 General
Colonel	 Colonel
	Lieutenant Colonel
Major	Major
Captain	Captain
1st Lieutenant	1st Lieutenant
2nd Lieutenant	2nd Lieutenant

Both Union and Confederate Enlisted Men

 Sergeant Major   Sergeant   Corporal

As it became clear that the Civil War would not end quickly, the North and South realized that the weapons used by the U.S. Army were outdated. Both sides began to modernize weapons for their armies. They used technology to increase accuracy, distance, ease of use, and damage to the enemy.

New Technologies

Earlier smoothbore muskets propelled a bullet down a smooth barrel. Rifle-muskets had spiral grooves inside the barrel. The spirals created a spin that made the rifle shoot farther and with more accuracy. Another invention, the minié bullet, or ball, made rifles more practical. The minié expanded as it traveled down the spirals in the barrel, picking up speed. A trained infantryman could shoot three times a minute and carried about 40–80 rounds of ammunition.

COMMON CIVIL WAR WEAPONS

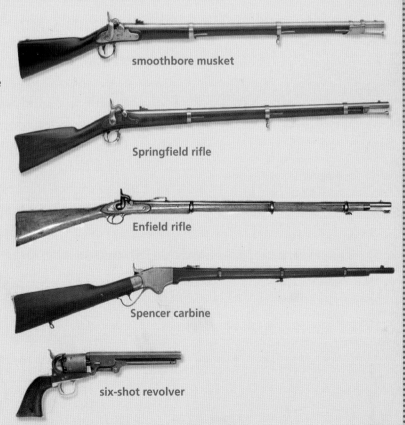

At the beginning of the war, smoothbore muskets were the most common weapon. By 1862, most soldiers used rifle-muskets.

By 1863, most soldiers on both sides had Springfields (made in Massachusetts) or Enfields (made in England). Both fired minié balls and were muzzle-loaded.

smoothbore musket

The .58 caliber Springfield rifle was one of the main weapons used by the infantry. The Union army ordered almost 1.2 million of them between 1861 and 1865.

Springfield rifle

The .57 caliber Enfield rifle was the other main weapon of the infantry.

Enfield rifle

The .56 caliber Spencer carbine was used by the Union cavalry. The infantry carried a Spencer rifle. These repeating rifles could fire seven shots before reloading.

Spencer carbine

Many pistols were used during the war. Some cavalrymen carried as many as six revolvers. Colt revolvers were the most common. Army and navy revolvers were different calibers.

six-shot revolver

Muskets were muzzle-loaded. This meant that only one bullet at a time could be loaded from the barrel, or front, of the gun. Manufacturers soon developed breech-loaded guns that allowed the user to insert a bullet and the powder needed to propel the bullet at the back of the gun. This made it easier and faster to load. The Union Army also used repeating rifles. These held many rounds of ammunition so a soldier could fire several times without reloading.

Weapons that were accurate at great distances benefited soldiers defending their position. Sharpshooters could aim at soldiers and horses from much farther away than ever before. This made artillery less effective because the soldiers couldn't drag it close enough. As a result, both sides had to change **tactics**. They relied less on artillery, which was used mostly for defense. Cavalry charges were made less often, as they often resulted in huge casualties. The minié ball and the rifle were a deadly combination.

The Navy

Both the North and the South were unprepared when war broke out. The Union navy was small but grew quickly as boats were built or bought. Starting with 42 active boats, the navy expanded to 671 by the end of the war. The steam-powered warships used in the blockade of the South were built so quickly they were called "90-day gunboats." Most shipbuilding yards and engineers were located in the North and they set to work building boats that could be used on the ocean, as well as boats for shallower inland waterways.

At the outset, the Confederacy did not have a navy but it did seize federal shipyards in the South when the states seceded. The Confederate navy also started outfitting itself. It built ironclads, which were low-lying steam-powered boats with armor. It bought boats from England to attack Union merchant ships carrying goods to Europe. It also developed new devices such as the first submarine to successfully sink a ship, underwater explosives, and torpedo boats.

The naval war was fought on two fronts. Ships fighting in the Atlantic Ocean and Gulf of Mexico were part of the "blue water navy." Ships fighting on the Mississippi River and other inland rivers were part of the "brown water navy." Each navy played an important role.

People in the War

Robert Smalls

Robert Smalls was an enslaved crewman on the Confederate ship *Planter*. On May 13, 1862, Smalls, his family, and some of the other slaves stole the ship. He then sailed the ship and turned the *Planter* over to the Union. He became a Northerner, freeing himself and his family. Smalls became an inspiration to other slaves.

Later, Smalls became the first black U.S. Navy captain. Congress also declared him as the "first hero" of the Civil War. After the war, Smalls served as a U.S. congressman.

The Ocean War

Early Union naval strategy was a blockade of the Southern ports. Union ships wanted to stop Southern trade with European countries. The Union hoped to cripple the Southern economy. At first, the North did not have enough ships to keep up the blockade. When the army and navy joined forces and captured the port of Hatteras in North Carolina, the blockade began working.

The Confederate strategy was to get around the blockade. The Confederacy went about this in two ways. The Confederate Navy attacked, looted, and destroyed Union merchant ships. They licensed private sailors to attack these ships, and allowed them to keep the goods they took. The South developed small, fast ships to run the blockade. These stealthy ships slipped by the Union blockade and brought goods into the South. Despite these efforts, the Union was able to reduce Southern trade by two-thirds, which significantly affected the Southern economy.

The River War

Once the Union occupied New Orleans, it worked toward the goal of controlling the Mississippi River from the Gulf of Mexico to Cairo, Illinois. This would cut off the South on its western side, as the blockade isolated it to the east and south. It would also allow the Union to easily move troops and supplies deep into Southern territory.

Confederate forts were located along the Mississippi, Tennessee, and Cumberland rivers. Union shipbuilders designed shallow steam-powered ships to operate in these waters. The ships were outfitted with **rudders** at both ends so they could move quickly in either direction. To defend themselves from artillery, the ships were covered in armor.

At Fort Henry and Fort Donelson, the Union navy and army worked together to attack Confederate forts from land as well as water. The navy guns protected army troops as they landed south of Vicksburg to begin the siege that would end in cutting the South in two.

Life as a Sailor

Like the soldiers on land, sailors spent a small amount of time in battle. They had many daily tasks to keep the ships running. They still suffered from boredom, though. Sailors did the same kinds of activities as soldiers. They played cards and board games. Singing was popular. Sailors also spent a lot of time writing letters home.

Notable Civil War Navy Ships

IRONCLADS Ironclads were ships encased in armor. Confederates built the first ironclad of the war. They took a ruined U.S. ship, the *Merrimack*, covered it in thick iron plates, and renamed it the *Virginia*. The Union soon built its own ironclad, the *Monitor*. When the two ships faced off, it was a draw. Over the course of the war, both sides built and used more ironclads.

RIVER GUNBOATS "Pook's turtles" were ironclad river gunboats. The boats were designed by another engineer, but Pook designed the casing that sheltered the crew and machinery. It looked like a turtle shell and was christened "Pook's turtles" by the sailors. These boats had flat bottoms, which allowed them to easily navigate inland rivers.

Top to bottom: the ironclad Merrimack*; a Union ironclad river gunboat; the submarine* H.L. Hunley*; and (lower right) Confederate mines or barrel torpedoes*

THE FIRST SUBMARINE The Confederate submarine *H.L. Hunley* was the first submarine in history to sink an enemy warship in battle. Unfortunately, it sunk immediately after. The sub was located in waters off of Charleston, South Carolina, in 1995. It was raised to the surface in 2000.

The *H.L. Hunley* and the "David" class torpedo boats carried a "spar" torpedo partly underwater on the front. It was an explosive charge on a long shaft. The torpedo boat rammed the charge into another ship, then set off the explosive.

MINES The Confederate Torpedo Corps laid mines in rivers and ports. Mines were usually made from sheets of iron filled with gunpowder. It would explode when touched by a ship. Confederate mines sunk 27 Union ships during the war.

THE IRON-PLATED REBEL STEAMER "MERRIMAC."

Communications

The vast area and large size of the armies involved in the Civil War made communicating a challenge. Resources such as railroads, telegraphs, and steamboats were used. New methods such as hot air balloons and signaling with flags were used. Even the traditional cavalry changed to become more a way to communicate than to fight.

Telegraph

The telegraph was an important tool during the Civil War. Telegraph messages were sent electronically using a system of dashes and dots that signified each letter of the alphabet, called Morse Code. It allowed people to communicate easily and quickly. It also allowed messages to travel over great distances. Lincoln often used the White House telegraph to talk with commanders in the field. In 1861, the Union established the U.S. Military Telegraph Corps. This corps trained thousands of telegraph operators. It was responsible for sending and receiving millions of messages. The Union army strung more than 15,000 miles [24,000 km] of telegraph wires during the war.

The Confederate telegraph service lagged behind the Union. Only 10 percent of the 50,000 miles (80,500 km) of telegraph wire in the United States in 1861 was located in the South. During the war, the South built only 1,000 miles (1,600 km). There was no official government telegraph service. The Confederacy relied instead on private companies run by civilians. It was not easy to repair or replace damaged wires and poles. Telegraph operators were in danger of capture by Union soldiers. In spite of this, the telegraph was very important. It was used to transfer battle orders to and from the Confederate government, as well as relay frontline news to newspaper editors to share with people at home.

Balloons

Hot air balloons were used during the Civil War to scout for information. The Union formed a Union Army Balloon Corps. The Confederates also experimented with using balloons, but not as much

Soldiers climbed to the top of a signal tower to see and send signals up to 15 miles (24 km) away.

"…*the men of the Signal Service were risking their lives in the forefront of battle, speeding orders of advance, warnings of impending danger*…"

—Union Chief Signal Officer of the Army, Major General Irving J. Carr as the North. Overall, the balloons were not used that much on either side, but they proved to be valuable for observing from the air.

Signaling

Union Lieutenant Albert J. Myer developed a type of communication called "wig-wag" signaling. Soldiers used a flag to send signals. At night, sometimes they would use a torch. Confederate Edward Porter Alexander made wig-wag signaling popular in the South. Both the North and South had its own Signal Corps.

The Wounded

Advances in weaponry unfortunately resulted in terrible battle wounds. Minié balls caused many of the worst wounds. They splintered bones and stayed inside the body instead of passing through it. Sadly, advancements in medicine did not keep pace with advancements in weaponry.

Medicine

At the time of the Civil War, medicine was still quite primitive. Doctors and nurses had no knowledge of germs. As a result, doctors did not keep their operating instruments sterile. They often searched for bullets with their fingers and held operating instruments in their mouths. Doctors had no disinfectants or antibiotics. Wounds often became infected, and infections often spread.

Modern painkillers or anesthetics had not yet been developed. Ether and chloroform were used to make a patient unconscious. When doctors ran out of these, soldiers were given whiskey. Morphine was available, but it was often in short supply, especially in the South. Soldiers often had no painkillers after amputations.

> " *The house was full of the wounded. They had taken our sitting room as an operating room, and our piano served as an amputating table...*
>
> —Sue Chancellor, a Southern girl "

People in the War

Jonathan Letterman

Dr. Jonathan Letterman became the Medical Director of the Army of the Potomac in 1862. He was called "the father of battlefield medicine" because of his many improvements to battlefield medicine. Some of his accomplishments include:

- the first dedicated Ambulance Corps
- the first system to sort victims in order of priority, called the *triage system*
- an evacuation system to get the wounded off the battlefields and treated efficiently
- an improved distribution system for medical supplies

Doctors

Civil War doctors did not receive the type of training modern doctors do. In addition, anyone could be called a doctor, even if they had no training at all. The soldiers did not trust doctors. Soldiers sometimes hid illnesses and wounds so they could avoid the doctors and hospital. They called the doctors "quacks" and "butchers." Doctors were also called "sawbones" because of the number of amputations they performed.

AMBULANCES

One medical advance during the Civil War was the ambulance service. By 1862, the Union created a trained, dedicated Ambulance Corps to reliably transport the wounded away from battle. The Confederacy developed a similar "Infirmary Corps" the same year, but on a smaller scale. As a result, the armies were able to quickly evacuate the wounded from battles.

Amputations

Doctors only knew one way to fix many wounds: amputation. Three out of four operations were amputations. A soldier's chance of survival depended on where he was hurt. The farther away the wound was from the trunk of the body, the better the chance of survival.

Hospitals

At the beginning of the war, wounded men were often left without medical attention for days. Medical procedures changed, fortunately. The wounded were first evaluated, then treated. First, they went to a dressing station near the battle for treatment. If they needed further help, they were taken to a field hospital. This was where amputations generally took place.

A field hospital could be located in a barn, house, tent, or open area. An operating table might be made from a door resting on two barrels. After being treated at the field hospital, soldiers would be taken to a hospital away from the fighting.

Statistics on Amputations

Type of Amputation	Number of Cases	Number of Deaths	Percentage of Deaths
Hand or fingers	7,902	198	2.9
In upper arm	5,510	1,273	23.8
At shoulder joint	866	245	29.1
Foot or toes	1,519	81	5.7
In leg	5,523	1,790	33.2
In thigh	6,369	3,411	54.2
At hip joint	66	55	83.3

Source: *The Library of Congress Civil War Desk Reference*

In the table, note the increase in percentage of deaths as the wounds get closer to the trunk of the body.

African Americans and Women

The majority of Civil War soldiers and sailors were white men, but they were not the only ones to make a difference in the war. Two groups made particularly important contributions: African Americans and women.

African Americans in the Civil War

Enslaved people made up about 30 percent of the South's population. Southerners did not want slaves to serve as soldiers. They were afraid the slaves would use their weapons to revolt. As a result, enslaved people were only used in roles such as laborers, cooks, and nurses. Near the end of the war, the Confederacy became desperate. In March 1865, the Confederate Congress passed a law that allowed slaves to fight, but the war ended before the law could go into effect.

African Americans were allowed to join the U.S. Navy to fight for the Union. They had played an important part in the War of 1812 and the Mexican War. African Americans were not allowed to enlist in the Union until 1862. Even when they couldn't fight, they joined the army in support roles such as servants and wagon drivers. Also, some escaped slaves became guides and spies.

As the war progressed, more soldiers were needed. The Union finally accepted all the African Americans who wanted to fight.

What Do You Know!

ENDING SLAVERY

Lincoln issued the Emancipation Proclamation on January 1, 1863. It freed all the slaves in the Confederacy. By that time, about 100,000 slaves had already fled the South. The Proclamation encouraged even more slaves to run away to the North. It also resulted in thousands of African Americans enlisting in the Union army.

In 1865, the U.S. Congress passed the Thirteenth Amendment to the Constitution. This officially freed all enslaved people in the United States.

In 1862, Congress passed a law allowing African Americans to join the army. In May 1863, the Bureau of Colored Troops was created. As a result, African Americans could volunteer or be drafted to fight. African-American regiments were made of all African-American troops. Usually, white men were the officers. These African-American troops were called the U.S. Colored Troops, or U.S.C.T.

Life as an African-American Soldier

African-American soldiers faced the same struggles that white soldiers did, including disease and poor food. They had several other challenges that white soldiers did not have to face.

Overcoming Racism

Not all white Union soldiers were happy about African Americans serving in the Union army. African-American soldiers faced racism from their fellow Union soldiers.

African-American soldiers were sometimes kept from fighting. Instead, they were assigned work duties, performing tasks such as digging trenches, burying the dead, and guarding the forts. Over time, white attitudes changed as African-American soldiers repeatedly showed their bravery in battle. As the war progressed, many white soldiers began to appreciate them.

> " *The colored troops are very highly valued here and there is no apparent difference in the way they are treated... The truth is they have fought their way into the respect of all the army.* "
>
> —U.S.C.T. officer Lewis Weld, August 17, 1864

> " *It is no longer possible to doubt the bravery and steadiness of the colored race...* "
>
> —*The New York Times*, about African Americans fighting at the Battle of Port Hudson, June 1863

Men of the 4th U.S. Colored Infantry at Fort Lincoln, 1865

People in the War

William Carney

Sergeant William Carney was the first of 26 African Americans to receive the Medal of Honor in the Civil War. Carney was a member of the 54th Massachusetts Regiment. During the battle at Fort Wagner in 1863, Carney was shot through the thigh. He continued on, crawling on his knees, carrying the Union flag, and encouraging his troops to follow him. He received the Medal of Honor for "most distinguished gallantry in action."

Public opinion in the North was also divided about the use of African-American soldiers. Some racist attitudes changed over time, however. At the battle of Port Hudson in 1863, African-American troops showed such courage that they won public support for all of the U.S.C.T.

Pay

When African Americans were first allowed to serve the Union as soldiers in 1862, they were paid $10 per month. White soldiers were paid $13 per month. In 1863, the U.S. War Department began deducting $3 from the pay of African-American soldiers to pay for uniforms, although white soldiers did not pay for theirs. African-American soldiers did not have the option of quitting the military.

Some African-American soldiers refused their pay until they were paid the same as regular soldiers. Unfortunately, it was not until June 1864 that they got equal pay. African-American soldiers in the Union navy did not have these problems. They received equal pay throughout the war.

The Confederate Threat

When African-American soldiers did fight, they faced added dangers. By 1863, Confederate President Davis and the Confederate Congress had issued harsh laws against African-American soldiers and their white officers. These laws allowed for their trial and execution if captured.

Southern troops sometimes specifically targeted African-American soldiers. At Fort Pillow in 1864, Confederate soldiers killed African-American soldiers after they had surrendered. "Remember Fort Pillow!" became a rallying cry for African-American soldiers. In another example, at the 1865 Battle of the Crater, Confederate soldiers focused on shooting the officers and the African-American soldiers. As a result, the African-American soldiers suffered 40 percent of the casualties.

Effectiveness

African-American troops proved to be a huge help to the North. They swelled the Union's ranks. Seeing African Americans in battle also gave hope to slaves in the South and encouraged them to flee and fight for the North. African Americans fought in over 40 major battles and many other minor ones. Some regiments, like the 54th Massachusetts, became famous for their heroism.

> *I have been one of those men who never had much confidence in colored troops fighting, but those doubts are now all removed, for they fought as bravely as any troops in the fort.*
>
> —Union Colonel S.G. Hicks, after the Battle of Fort Pillow, March 25, 1864

Beyond the War

By the end of the war, about 179,000 African-American soldiers had served in the Union army. They made up roughly ten percent of the army's soldiers. About 18,000 African-American men served in the U.S. Navy. This was about 15 percent of those who served. Eighteen African-American soldiers and eight African-American sailors received the **Medal of Honor** for their bravery.

Life for African Americans after the war improved in numerous ways. Many soldiers in the U.S.C.T. moved into leadership positions, including jobs as legislators, lieutenant governors, and congressmen. In 1866, Congress passed the Fourteenth Amendment. This granted full citizenship to anyone born in the United States, including African Americans. African Americans were able to vote when the Fifteenth Amendment became a law in 1870.

Although they made progress, African Americans continued to experience many difficulties. Though slavery had ended, some Southern states instituted **black codes**, which were unfair laws that returned many African Americans to slave-like conditions. Also, the U.S. government did not keep all its promises. For example, in 1865, General Sherman's Field Order No. 15 promised freed African Americans 40 acres (160,200 m²) of land and a mule. When President Andrew Johnson took office, many of the African Americans were evicted from their land, and it was returned to the former white owners.

Women in the Civil War

With the men away fighting, women took on new roles during the Civil War. They found several important ways to help in the war effort.

People in the War

Walt Whitman

Famous American poet Walt Whitman was a male nurse in the Civil War. On learning that his brother was wounded in a battle, he rushed to Maryland to see him. Fortunately, his brother's wound was not serious. Whitman visited other injured soldiers and was asked if he would help in the hospitals in Washington. Whitman agreed and became a nurse. He wrote about his experience in the poetry book *The Wound Dresser.*

Louisa May Alcott

Nurses

All nurses were men at the beginning of the war. Nursing was considered a dangerous occupation and not entirely appropriate for women. Many people thought women should not be exposed to the horrors of war, disease, and death. As the war continued and casualties began to mount, this attitude changed.

In the South, women formed volunteer groups. These groups raised money and helped set up hospitals. Women expanded this role in 1862, when the Confederate Congress passed a law allowing women nurses in the army hospitals.

In the North, several women's groups joined together to form the U.S. Sanitary Commission in 1861. It raised money and sent medical supplies and nurses to hospitals and camps. In 1862, the Union **Surgeon General** began asking that at least one-third of the nurses in hospitals be women.

In the North and South, female nurses were not welcome at first. Nurse Georgeanna Woolsey summarized the attitude of many surgeons:

"No one knows ... how much opposition, how much ill-will, how much unfeeling want of thought, these women nurses endured. Hardly a surgeon whom I can think of received or treated them with even common courtesy. Government had decided that women should be employed, and the Army surgeons—unable, therefore to close the hospitals against them—determined to make their lives so unbearable that they should be forced in self-defense to leave."

Eventually, there were about 3,200 paid nurses on both sides, and many more unpaid.

LOUISA MAY ALCOTT Alcott paused in her career as a writer to enlist as a nurse. She summed up the attitude of many female nurses when she wrote, "I long to be a man, but as I can't fight, I will content myself with working for those who can."

CLARA BARTON Known as the "Angel of the Battlefield," Barton braved active battles to bring soldiers food and supplies and to help the wounded. After the war, she organized the **American Red Cross** and became its first president. She wrote about tending the wounded: "We are waiting at the cotside and closing their eyes one by one as they pass away… I cannot but think that we shall win at last, but oh the cost…."

MARY ANN BICKERDYKE Bickerdyke took charge and improved conditions wherever she went. "Mother Bickerdyke" got the Union soldiers food and supplies, and she cleaned up the camps and hospitals. Sherman respected her so much that she was the only woman he allowed in his advance hospitals. She rode at the head of Sherman's Fifteenth Army Corps in the Grand Army Review in Washington, DC, at the end of the war.

KATE CUMMING Like many women, Cumming's family felt nursing was inappropriate for a lady. Despite their disapproval, Cumming became one of the South's top matrons and nurses. Summing up the experience of many nurses, she wrote, "Nothing that I had ever heard or read had given me the faintest idea of the horrors witnessed here."

DOROTHEA DIX Dix convinced the army to create the first female Nursing Corps. She became superintendent of female nurses in the Union army. After the war, Dix worked to improve the care of the mentally ill.

ELLA KING NEWSOM Known as "the Florence Nightingale of the South," Newsom was in charge of several hospitals in the South.

SUSIE KING TAYLOR Taylor worked as a nurse and laundress for the U.S.C.T. She was the only African-American woman to publish a book about her experience in the war.

Mary Ann Bickerdyke

Dorthea Dix

On the Front Lines

Women also found other ways to serve. Some women became camp followers and traveled with the soldiers. They were usually laundresses and cooks. Others formed relief organizations that collected food, clothing, and medical supplies. They also made uniforms and bandages.

Some women actually fought in the war. More than 400 women disguised themselves as men so they could serve as soldiers. Jennie Hodgers, one of the most famous, served under the name Albert Cashier. She fought in more than 40 battles over three years.

A few women fought without disguising themselves. For example, Kady Brownell followed her husband into the war and became a **color-bearer** for his company. She helped him and several other soldiers to safety when they were wounded.

Clara Barton

People in the War

Dr Mary Edwards Walker

Mary Edwards Walker was one of the few female doctors of the Civil War period. At first, Walker was not allowed to work in the war as a doctor. Instead, she volunteered as a nurse. Later, she was hired as an assistant surgeon in the 52nd Ohio Infantry—the first female surgeon in the army. After the war, she became the first woman to earn the Medal of Honor.

Spies

Some women served as spies. Belle Boyd became known as the "Cleopatra of the Confederacy." Among other things, she warned General Jackson about the Union's Shenandoah Valley plans. Rose O'Neal Greenhow, another very successful Southern spy, had a whole network of contacts and messengers. She was able to warn the South about the North's attack at Manassas.

Belle Boyd, a spy, was called "Cleopatra of the Confederacy."

The North also had its female spies. Harriet Tubman was one of the most famous. In addition to her work helping to rescue slaves and as a nurse, Tubman was also a spy. She went behind enemy lines and scouted for the Union. Pauline Cushman was known as "The Spy of Cumberland." Cushman used her talents as an actress to gather information and pass it to the Union. Some women disguised themselves as men to spy. Both Sarah Edmonds (Union) and Loretta Janeta Velázquez (Confederate) dressed as men and were spies as well as soldiers.

After the War

The Civil War somewhat redefined the role of women. By the end of the war, thousands of women had served as nurses, changing the medical field forever. Plus, some jobs, such as nursing, that had been considered improper for women were now acceptable. Women even gained the **reluctant** respect of some of their male peers during the war.

The women's rights movement had begun before the war. After the war, the Fifteenth Amendment was passed giving voting rights to African Americans, but women still could not vote. With all they had accomplished in the war, and with these new rights being passed, women were encouraged more than ever to fight for the right to vote.

5 *Prisoners of War*

Both the Union and the Confederacy captured thousands of prisoners. Neither side had good plans for dealing with them, though. As a result, caring for and managing prisoners became a huge problem.

Prisoner Exchanges

Neither the North nor the South expected the war to last very long. At first neither side had enough prison facilities. By 1862, both sides had thousands of prisoners. In July 1862, the North and South struck the Dix-Hill deal. In this deal, both sides agreed to exchange prisoners. The exchange, or cartel, was based on rank. Privates and common seamen were the smallest unit of exchange, and generals and admirals were the largest (see table).

Sometimes, however, one side had more prisoners than the other. In that case, the extra prisoners were **paroled**. This meant they were sent back to their own side. They had to agree not to perform any military duties, including fighting, until their side evened out the exchange. At first, this system was a success. By August 1862, the prisons on both sides had been mostly emptied.

Prisoner Exchange Rates	
Officer Rank	*Privates or Seamen Needed for Exchange*
General or Admiral	60
Flag Officer or Major General	40
Commodore or Brigadier-General	20
Navy Captain or Colonel	15
Lieutenant-Colonel or Navy	10
Lieutenant Commander or Major	8
Privates or Common Seamen	1

Source: *The Library of Congress Civil War Desk Reference*

Exchange Problems

Problems quickly arose with the exchange system. The Union accused the South of letting paroled prisoners fight before they should have been allowed to. The South accused the North of holding regular citizens as prisoners of war. Still, the prisoner exchange system worked until 1863. Two main issues halted the prisoner exchanges.

First, the North and South could not agree on how to treat African-American prisoners of war. When Lincoln made the Emancipation Proclamation, African-American troops joined the war. In response, the South passed laws allowing African-American soldiers to be enslaved or executed if captured, and their white officers could be hung. The North wanted African-Americans to be treated the same as other soldiers.

Second, Confederate and Union officials could not agree on how many men had been paroled or exchanged. Confederate officials claimed that the paroles of Confederate soldiers were not valid because they had been done incorrectly. They returned most of their paroled soldiers to duty.

Attempts were made to get the exchange working again, but neither side would budge on the issue of the African-American prisoners. As a result, by fall 1863, the prisoner exchange system was halted.

Renewed Exchanges

With no more mass exchanges, prisons rapidly filled up. By 1864, the Northern public began pressuring Lincoln to renew exchanges. The South would not budge on the African-American issue, so no progress was made.

In October 1864, the Confederate and Union governments agreed to allow food and supplies to be sent to prisoners. Then in January 1865,

What Do You Know!

ESCAPE ARTISTS

Although prison escapes were rare, a few were managed by both sides. Union soldiers Colonel Thomas E. Rose and Major Andrew G. Hamilton were part of one of the most famous prison escapes of the Civil War. They and over 100 other prisoners escaped Libby Prison in the South. They spent 47 days digging an escape tunnel.

Confederate General John Hunt Morgan made his own escape. He and six others escaped from the Ohio State Penitentiary, also by tunneling their way out.

> *It is hard on our men held in Southern prisons not to exchange them, but it is humanity to those left in the ranks to fight our battles. Every man we hold, when released on parole or otherwise, becomes an active soldier against us at once either directly or indirectly.*
>
> —General Grant, to General Butler, August 18, 1864

the South finally agreed to exchange all prisoners, including African Americans. By February, exchanges began again. Before the exchanges were complete, however, the war ended.

Union prisoners of war at Andersonville prison camp

Prisons

When the exchange system broke down in 1863, prisons in the North and South quickly became crowded. The prisons were not built to handle such large numbers of men. Most prisons were quickly and poorly built. They ranged from warehouse-style buildings to fenced-in open areas. Some were meant for the short-term, while others were used for years. During the war, there were over 150 war prisons.

Conditions in prisons on both sides were terrible. The prisons were very unclean and unhealthy. Prisoners suffered from hunger and disease. The food and water was often toxic and medical care was lacking. Conditions were a little better in the North where prisoners had at least some type of shelter from barracks or tents. In the South, the prisoners sometimes had no shelter at all.

Andersonville Prison in Georgia

Andersonville, also called Camp Sumter, is widely considered to be the worst of the Civil War prisons. Designed to hold 10,000 prisoners, it held around 33,000 at its peak. The only source of water was a stream that quickly became polluted. The prison was simply a fenced-in area with no shelter. Prisoners would sometimes burrow into the ground to get shelter from the weather. They also built

> *[I] walk around camp every morning looking for acquaintances… Can see a dozen most any morning laying around dead.*
>
> —Brigade Quartermaster John L. Ransom, 9th Michigan Cavalry and prisoner at Andersonville

makeshift shelters out of blankets and sticks. Still, many died of exposure. During one hot August, more than 100 Andersonville prisoners died each day. In addition to exposure, prisoners died of disease and malnutrition. By the end of the war, about 13,000 of the camp's prisoners had died.

Elmira Prison in New York

Nicknamed "Helmira," Elmira was considered to be the worst prison in the North. It had the highest death rate of any Union prison and about 24 percent of its prisoner population died. Like Andersonville, its water was polluted. The prisoners suffered from disease, malnutrition, and exposure. Instead of baking in the summer heat, Elmira prisoners froze during the winter cold. Also, Elmira also had the unusual distinction of having tourists, as civilians paid to look over the prison walls.

African-American Prisoners of War

African-American soldiers captured by the South had a much more difficult time than white soldiers. Some were killed after they surrendered. Others were returned to their former owners or sold to new ones. If they made it to prison, African-American soldiers often received harsher treatment from the guards. They were put to hard labor and given jobs such as latrine duty and burial detail.

Mistreatment and Deaths

Both sides accused each other of mistreating prisoners of war. In particular, many in the North claimed the South purposely tortured prisoners in places such as Andersonville. People who have studied the Civil War generally agree that this was not the case. A shortage of resources was mainly to blame for the miserable conditions. The South could not feed and shelter its own people, so there were few resources for prisoners of war.

By the end of the war, the deaths on both sides were high. Of the 194,743 Union prisoners of war, 30,218 (15.5 percent) died in Southern prisons.

THE SULTANA DISASTER

After the war ended, the government began sending home the prisoners of war. On April 27, 1865, the *Sultana* steamboat was transporting prisoners from Cahaba and Andersonville prison. Disaster struck on the Mississippi near Memphis, Tennessee. This boat was designed to hold 376 people but, on that day, it had more than 2,000. This was too much weight for the boat. As a result, the boilers on the *Sultana* exploded and about 1,500–1,700 people were killed.

Of the 214,865 Confederate prisoners of war, 25,976 (12 percent) died in Northern prisons.

Conclusion

The Civil War changed the way soldiers lived and fought during war. These changes affected many people, including women and African Americans.

AFRICAN AMERICANS IN THE ARMED FORCES The role of African Americans in the military continued to change over the next century. Many Civil War veterans fought in the Indian wars throughout the late 1800s. They came to be called "Buffalo Soldiers."

African Americans continued to serve in the military but were still grouped in all-black regiments. That changed over time and, by 1953, 95 percent of the army's African-American soldiers were in **integrated** units that included soldiers of all races. As of 2008, almost 20 percent of the active army was African American.

Male (above) and female African-American soldiers in today's Army

WOMEN IN THE ARMED FORCES After the Civil War, the role of women in the military continued to grow. Female nurses continue to serve a huge role in wars. Female doctors have increased also. In World War I, 35,000 women had noncombat military jobs. In World War II, women served as pilots in the Women's Army Corps. In 2009, more than 13 percent of the members of the active army were women.

PRISONERS OF WAR In 1869, Clara Barton went to Switzerland. There she learned about the Red Cross and the 1864 Geneva Convention. Among other things, this treaty guaranteed better treatment for wounded soldiers and prisoners of war. Barton worked hard to get the United States to sign this treaty. In 1882, she succeeded.

> *For more than two hundred years, African Americans have participated in every conflict in United States history. They have not only fought bravely the common enemies of the United States but have also had to confront the individual and institutional racism of their countrymen.*
>
> —Lt. Col. (Ret) Michael Lee Lanning, author, *The African-American Soldier: From Crispus Attucks to Colin Powell*

Today those helping the wounded are treated as neutrals on the battlefield.

Commenting on her struggles to get the United States to sign the Geneva Convention, Barton said, "(Every) civilized nation on the earth *but ours*, has signed... we alone class with the barbarians."

WOUNDED SOLDIERS The huge number of injuries in the Civil War served to advance medicine. Doctors learned more about how to treat wounds and diseases. Hospitals for soldiers also improved.

During the war, medical workers began to be treated as **neutrals**. In other words, soldiers would not shoot at doctors, nurses, or orderlies. The 1864, Geneva Convention guaranteed protection for those helping the wounded. Today, there are several Geneva Conventions in place that make sure the wounded, as well as medical workers, are treated well during times of war.

Final Thoughts

Lincoln summed up his hopes for life after the Civil War in his second Inaugural Address:

> *"With malice toward none; with charity for all; with firmness in the right, as God gives us to see the right, let us strive on to finish the work we are in; to bind up the nation's wounds; to care for him who shall have borne the battle, and for his widow, and his orphan—to do all which may achieve and cherish a just and lasting peace among ourselves, and with all nations."*

—President Abraham Lincoln, March 4, 1865

The Civil War affected almost every American. It changed the way Americans fought and lived during wartime. It also changed how society thought about women and African Americans, paving the way for future social changes. The Civil War brought about medical advancements that would save the lives of soldiers in later wars. These included a way of managing large numbers of wounded through a system of field hospitals and the importance of sanitation. These are a few good things that came about from four tragic years in United States history.

GLOSSARY

abolitionist A person who argued for the end of slavery in the United States

American Red Cross A humanitarian organization of volunteers founded by Clara Barton in 1881

artillery Large guns that are usually mounted on a carriage so they can be moved from place to place and fired a long distance at enemy positions

black codes Unfair laws enacted in Southern states after the Civil War for the purpose of returning African Americans to slave-like conditions

blockade To use hostile ships to close off trade

bombproof A type of shelter made by soldiers, constructed of wood and dirt

bounty A payment offered to men who volunteered to fight

brigade A large group of soldiers, made up of four regiments

butternuts Nickname for Confederate soldiers and their uniforms, referring to the dye used to color the cloth

camp The place where soldiers lived, slept, and ate together

casualties A loss in the fighting strength of a military unit due to causes such as wounds or death

cavalry A branch of the army that rode horses

color-bearer The person who carries the flag for his company or regiment

commutation Paying a fee to avoid serving in the military

company A military unit of 50-100 soldiers

confederation A group of individual states that agree to work together on some issues but keep their independence in other areas

conscription Laws requiring men to serve in the military

contaminate To make something unclean and possibly harmful

crude Rough and lacking in completeness

diarrhea Abnormally frequent evacuation of the intestines with more or less liquid stools

dog tent A common type of tent that soldiers used for shelter

draft A process of selecting men to serve in the military

drill The practice of military actions such as handling and firing weapons and marching

dysentery A disease characterized by severe diarrhea

enlist To volunteer for military service

exempted Excused from military service

forage To look for food and supplies often by looting the homes and farms of civilians

hardtack Hard crackers that were common food for Northern soldiers

haversack A canvas bag that carried a soldier's extra clothing and food

hygiene Cleanliness

immigrant A person who moves to another country to live permanently

Glossary

immune system A network of cells and tissues that keep a person healthy

infantry Soldiers who fight on foot and carry their own gear and weapons

insignia A symbol indicating military rank

integrate To bring diverse groups together

knapsack A leather bag that carried a soldier's gear and belongings

latrine A toilet

Medal of Honor The highest U.S. military award given by Congress for bravery in combat

military strategy Plans for conducting warfare including the movement of armed forces in relation to an enemy

militia A unit of citizen soldiers within a state often called upon during emergencies

morale The attitude of the troops

neutral An individual, state, or nation that chooses not to take sides in a war or political conflict

parole Freedom given to a prisoner of war in exchange for a promise that he would not fight

preserve To keep or maintain

rampage To behave violently

rank Position in the military, such as a private or captain

ration A fixed amount of food provided to civilians or military personnel

regiment A unit made up of about 1,000 men within the army

reluctant An unwillingness to do something

rudder A device used to steer a boat

rural Relating to the countryside

secede To leave the United States and form the Confederate States of America

shebang A temporary shelter built out of whatever was available

substitute A man paid to take the place of another man who had been drafted

Surgeon General The head of medical services of the U.S. Army

tactics A plan to achieve a goal

terrain A stretch of land, particularly its physical features

typhoid fever An infectious disease characterized by fever, diarrhea, and intestinal inflammation, caused by bacteria

MORE INFORMATION

Books

Bolotin, Norman. *Civil War A to Z: A Young Person's Guide to Over 100 People, Places, and Points of Importance.* Dutton Children's Books, 2002.

Chang, Ina. *A Separate Battle: Women And the Civil War.* Puffin, 1996.

Elliot, Henry. *Frederick Douglass: From Slavery to Statesman.* Crabtree Publishing Company, 2010.

Gay, Kathlyn. *Civil War.* Twenty-First Century Books, 1996.

Stanchak, John. *Civil War.* DK Publishing, 2011.

Varhola, Michael J. *Everyday Life During the Civil War.* Cincinnati: Writers Digest Books, 1999.

Volo, Dorothy Denneen, and James M. Volo. *Daily Life in Civil War America.* The Greenwood Press, 2010.

Wagner, Margaret E., Gary W. Gallagher, and Paul Finkelman. *The Library of Congress Civil War Desk Reference.* Simon & Schuster, 2002.

Websites

www.army.mil/africanamericans/timeline.html
Official U.S. Army site. Provides a timeline, profiles, and resources on African Americans in the U.S. Army.

www.army.mil/women/
Official U.S. Army site. Provides history, profiles, resources, and current information on women in the U.S. Army.

http://civilwar.org/
In-depth information on the Civil War. Provides a history center, videos, maps, a glossary, primary sources, and biographies. Teacher resources include classroom projects, presentations, and handouts.

http://ehistory.osu.edu/osu/default.cfm
Ohio State University History Department's site. Provides primary sources, book reviews, multimedia histories, maps, images, and timelines.

www.pbs.org/wgbh/amex/reconstruction/index.html
Official site of the film *Reconstruction: The Second Civil War.* Provides information on the Reconstruction era from 1863–1877. Includes a teacher's guide and questions and answers with historians.

About the Author

J. Matteson Claus is a writer and editor of books, audio books, and educational materials for grades 2-12.

INDEX